PADDLE BOA

LOG BOOK

THIS BOOK BELONGS TO:

_____

_____

_____

PAGE	JOURNEY NAME
1	
2	
3	
4	
5	
6	
7	
8	
9	
10	
11	
12	
13	
14	
15	
16	
17	
18	
19	
20	
21	
22	
23	
24	
25	

PAGE	JOURNEY NAME
26	
27	
28	
29	
30	
31	
32	
33	
34	
35	
36	
37	
38	
39	
40	
41	
42	
43	
44	
45	
46	
47	
48	
49	
50	

PAGE	JOURNEY NAME
51	
52	
53	
54	
55	
56	
57	
58	
59	
60	
61	
62	
63	
64	
65	
66	
67	
68	
69	
70	
71	
72	
73	
74	
75	

PAGE	JOURNEY NAME
76	
77	
78	
79	
80	
81	
82	
83	
84	
85	
86	
87	
88	
89	
90	
91	
92	
93	
94	
95	
96	
97	
98	
99	
100	

JOURNEY NAME _____

START DATE _____   END DATE _____

COMPANIONS _____

_____

_____

LOCATION _____

WEATHER CONDITIONS _____

_____

TRIP GOALS _____

_____

ROUTE _____

_____

_____

DISTANCE _____   TIME ON THE WATER _____

NOTES

_____
_____
_____
_____
_____
_____
_____
_____
_____
_____
_____
_____
_____
_____
_____
_____
_____

JOURNEY NAME _____

START DATE _____   END DATE _____

COMPANIONS _____

_____

_____

LOCATION _____

WEATHER CONDITIONS _____

_____

TRIP GOALS _____

_____

ROUTE _____

_____

_____

DISTANCE _____   TIME ON THE WATER _____

NOTES

_____
_____
_____
_____
_____
_____
_____
_____
_____
_____
_____
_____
_____
_____
_____
_____
_____
_____
_____

JOURNEY NAME _____

START DATE _____   END DATE _____

COMPANIONS _____
_____
_____

LOCATION _____

WEATHER CONDITIONS _____
_____

TRIP GOALS _____
_____

ROUTE _____
_____
_____

DISTANCE _____   TIME ON THE WATER _____

NOTES

_____
_____
_____
_____
_____
_____
_____
_____
_____
_____
_____
_____
_____
_____
_____
_____
_____
_____
_____
_____

JOURNEY NAME _____

START DATE _____   END DATE _____

COMPANIONS _____

_____

_____

LOCATION _____

WEATHER CONDITIONS _____

_____

TRIP GOALS _____

_____

ROUTE _____

_____

_____

DISTANCE _____   TIME ON THE WATER _____

NOTES

JOURNEY NAME _____

START DATE _____ END DATE _____

COMPANIONS _____

_____

_____

LOCATION _____

WEATHER CONDITIONS _____

_____

TRIP GOALS _____

_____

ROUTE _____

_____

_____

DISTANCE _____ TIME ON THE WATER _____

NOTES

JOURNEY NAME _____

START DATE _____   END DATE _____

COMPANIONS _____

_____

_____

LOCATION _____

WEATHER CONDITIONS _____

_____

TRIP GOALS _____

_____

ROUTE _____

_____

_____

DISTANCE _____   TIME ON THE WATER _____

NOTES

_____
_____
_____
_____
_____
_____
_____
_____
_____
_____
_____

_____
_____
_____
_____
_____
_____
_____
_____

JOURNEY NAME _____

START DATE _____ END DATE _____

COMPANIONS _____

_____

_____

LOCATION _____

WEATHER CONDITIONS _____

_____

TRIP GOALS _____

_____

ROUTE _____

_____

_____

DISTANCE _____ TIME ON THE WATER _____

NOTES

JOURNEY NAME _____

START DATE _____   END DATE _____

COMPANIONS _____

_____

_____

LOCATION _____

WEATHER CONDITIONS _____

_____

TRIP GOALS _____

_____

ROUTE _____

_____

_____

DISTANCE _____   TIME ON THE WATER _____

NOTES

_____
_____
_____
_____
_____
_____
_____
_____
_____
_____
_____

_____
_____
_____
_____
_____
_____
_____
_____
_____

JOURNEY NAME _____

START DATE _____   END DATE _____

COMPANIONS _____

_____

_____

LOCATION _____

WEATHER CONDITIONS _____

_____

TRIP GOALS _____

_____

ROUTE _____

_____

_____

DISTANCE _____   TIME ON THE WATER _____

NOTES

_____
_____
_____
_____
_____
_____
_____
_____
_____
_____
_____
_____
_____
_____
_____
_____
_____

JOURNEY NAME _____

START DATE _____   END DATE _____

COMPANIONS _____

_____

_____

LOCATION _____

WEATHER CONDITIONS _____

_____

TRIP GOALS _____

_____

ROUTE _____

_____

_____

DISTANCE _____   TIME ON THE WATER _____

NOTES

JOURNEY NAME _____

START DATE _____   END DATE _____

COMPANIONS _____

_____

_____

LOCATION _____

WEATHER CONDITIONS _____

_____

TRIP GOALS _____

_____

ROUTE _____

_____

_____

DISTANCE _____   TIME ON THE WATER _____

NOTES

JOURNEY NAME _____

START DATE _____ END DATE _____

COMPANIONS _____

_____

_____

LOCATION _____

WEATHER CONDITIONS _____

_____

TRIP GOALS _____

_____

ROUTE _____

_____

_____

DISTANCE _____ TIME ON THE WATER _____

NOTES

JOURNEY NAME _____

START DATE _____   END DATE _____

COMPANIONS _____

_____

_____

LOCATION _____

WEATHER CONDITIONS _____

_____

TRIP GOALS _____

_____

ROUTE _____

_____

_____

DISTANCE _____   TIME ON THE WATER _____

NOTES

JOURNEY NAME _____

START DATE _____ END DATE _____

COMPANIONS _____
_____
_____

LOCATION _____

WEATHER CONDITIONS _____
_____

TRIP GOALS _____
_____

ROUTE _____
_____
_____

DISTANCE _____ TIME ON THE WATER _____

NOTES

_____
_____
_____
_____
_____
_____
_____
_____
_____
_____
_____

JOURNEY NAME _____

START DATE _____   END DATE _____

COMPANIONS _____

_____

_____

LOCATION _____

WEATHER CONDITIONS _____

_____

TRIP GOALS _____

_____

ROUTE _____

_____

_____

DISTANCE _____   TIME ON THE WATER _____

NOTES

JOURNEY NAME _____

START DATE _____   END DATE _____

COMPANIONS _____

_____

_____

LOCATION _____

WEATHER CONDITIONS _____

_____

TRIP GOALS _____

_____

ROUTE _____

_____

_____

DISTANCE _____   TIME ON THE WATER _____

NOTES

JOURNEY NAME _____

START DATE _____ END DATE _____

COMPANIONS _____
_____
_____

LOCATION _____

WEATHER CONDITIONS _____
_____

TRIP GOALS _____
_____

ROUTE _____
_____
_____

DISTANCE _____ TIME ON THE WATER _____

NOTES

JOURNEY NAME _____

START DATE _____ END DATE _____

COMPANIONS _____

_____

_____

LOCATION _____

WEATHER CONDITIONS _____

_____

TRIP GOALS _____

_____

ROUTE _____

_____

_____

DISTANCE _____ TIME ON THE WATER _____

NOTES

_____
_____
_____
_____
_____
_____
_____
_____
_____
_____

_____
_____
_____
_____
_____
_____
_____
_____

JOURNEY NAME _____

START DATE _____   END DATE _____

COMPANIONS _____

_____

_____

LOCATION _____

WEATHER CONDITIONS _____

_____

TRIP GOALS _____

_____

ROUTE _____

_____

_____

DISTANCE _____   TIME ON THE WATER _____

NOTES

JOURNEY NAME _____

START DATE _____   END DATE _____

COMPANIONS _____

_____

_____

LOCATION _____

WEATHER CONDITIONS _____

_____

TRIP GOALS _____

_____

ROUTE _____

_____

_____

DISTANCE _____   TIME ON THE WATER _____

NOTES

_____

_____

_____

_____

_____

_____

_____

_____

_____

_____

_____

JOURNEY NAME _____

START DATE _____   END DATE _____

COMPANIONS _____

_____

_____

LOCATION _____

WEATHER CONDITIONS _____

_____

TRIP GOALS _____

_____

ROUTE _____

_____

_____

DISTANCE _____   TIME ON THE WATER _____

NOTES

JOURNEY NAME _____

START DATE _____   END DATE _____

COMPANIONS _____

_____

_____

LOCATION _____

WEATHER CONDITIONS _____

_____

TRIP GOALS _____

_____

ROUTE _____

_____

_____

DISTANCE _____   TIME ON THE WATER _____

NOTES

JOURNEY NAME _____

START DATE _____ END DATE _____

COMPANIONS _____
_____
_____

LOCATION _____

WEATHER CONDITIONS _____
_____

TRIP GOALS _____
_____

ROUTE _____
_____
_____

DISTANCE _____ TIME ON THE WATER _____

NOTES

JOURNEY NAME _____

START DATE _____ END DATE _____

COMPANIONS _____
_____
_____

LOCATION _____

WEATHER CONDITIONS _____
_____

TRIP GOALS _____
_____

ROUTE _____
_____
_____

DISTANCE _____ TIME ON THE WATER _____

NOTES

_____
_____
_____
_____
_____
_____
_____
_____
_____
_____
_____
_____
_____
_____
_____
_____
_____
_____

JOURNEY NAME _____

START DATE _____ END DATE _____

COMPANIONS _____

_____

_____

LOCATION _____

WEATHER CONDITIONS _____

_____

TRIP GOALS _____

_____

ROUTE _____

_____

_____

DISTANCE _____ TIME ON THE WATER _____

NOTES

_____

_____

_____

_____

_____

_____

_____

_____

_____

_____

_____

_____

_____

_____

_____

_____

_____

JOURNEY NAME _____

START DATE _____   END DATE _____

COMPANIONS _____

_____

_____

LOCATION _____

WEATHER CONDITIONS _____

_____

TRIP GOALS _____

_____

ROUTE _____

_____

_____

DISTANCE _____   TIME ON THE WATER _____

NOTES

_____
_____
_____
_____
_____
_____
_____
_____
_____
_____
_____
_____
_____
_____
_____
_____
_____
_____
_____

JOURNEY NAME _____

START DATE _____ END DATE _____

COMPANIONS _____
_____
_____

LOCATION _____

WEATHER CONDITIONS _____
_____

TRIP GOALS _____
_____

ROUTE _____
_____
_____

DISTANCE _____ TIME ON THE WATER _____

NOTES

_____
_____
_____
_____
_____
_____
_____
_____
_____
_____
_____
_____
_____
_____
_____
_____
_____
_____

JOURNEY NAME _____

START DATE _____   END DATE _____

COMPANIONS _____
_____
_____

LOCATION _____

WEATHER CONDITIONS _____
_____

TRIP GOALS _____
_____

ROUTE _____
_____
_____

DISTANCE _____   TIME ON THE WATER _____

NOTES

_____
_____
_____
_____
_____
_____
_____
_____
_____
_____
_____
_____
_____
_____
_____
_____
_____
_____

JOURNEY NAME _____

START DATE _____ END DATE _____

COMPANIONS _____

_____

_____

LOCATION _____

WEATHER CONDITIONS _____

_____

TRIP GOALS _____

_____

ROUTE _____

_____

_____

DISTANCE _____ TIME ON THE WATER _____

NOTES

JOURNEY NAME _____

START DATE _____   END DATE _____

COMPANIONS _____

_____

_____

LOCATION _____

WEATHER CONDITIONS _____

_____

TRIP GOALS _____

_____

ROUTE _____

_____

_____

DISTANCE _____   TIME ON THE WATER _____

NOTES

_____
_____
_____
_____
_____
_____
_____
_____
_____
_____

_____
_____
_____
_____
_____
_____
_____
_____

JOURNEY NAME _____

START DATE _____ END DATE _____

COMPANIONS _____

_____

_____

LOCATION _____

WEATHER CONDITIONS _____

_____

TRIP GOALS _____

_____

ROUTE _____

_____

_____

DISTANCE _____ TIME ON THE WATER _____

NOTES

JOURNEY NAME _____

START DATE _____   END DATE _____

COMPANIONS _____
_____
_____

LOCATION _____

WEATHER CONDITIONS _____
_____

TRIP GOALS _____
_____

ROUTE _____
_____
_____

DISTANCE _____   TIME ON THE WATER _____

NOTES

JOURNEY NAME _____

START DATE _____   END DATE _____

COMPANIONS _____

_____

_____

LOCATION _____

WEATHER CONDITIONS _____

_____

TRIP GOALS _____

_____

ROUTE _____

_____

_____

DISTANCE _____   TIME ON THE WATER _____

NOTES

_____
_____
_____
_____
_____
_____
_____
_____
_____
_____
_____
_____
_____
_____
_____
_____
_____

33

JOURNEY NAME _____

START DATE _____   END DATE _____

COMPANIONS _____

_____

_____

LOCATION _____

WEATHER CONDITIONS _____

_____

TRIP GOALS _____

_____

ROUTE _____

_____

_____

DISTANCE _____   TIME ON THE WATER _____

NOTES

JOURNEY NAME _____

START DATE _____   END DATE _____

COMPANIONS _____
_____
_____

LOCATION _____

WEATHER CONDITIONS _____
_____

TRIP GOALS _____
_____

ROUTE _____
_____
_____

DISTANCE _____   TIME ON THE WATER _____

NOTES

JOURNEY NAME _____

START DATE _____ END DATE _____

COMPANIONS _____
_____
_____

LOCATION _____

WEATHER CONDITIONS _____
_____

TRIP GOALS _____
_____

ROUTE _____
_____
_____

DISTANCE _____ TIME ON THE WATER _____

NOTES

JOURNEY NAME _____

START DATE _____ END DATE _____

COMPANIONS _____

_____

_____

LOCATION _____

WEATHER CONDITIONS _____

_____

TRIP GOALS _____

_____

ROUTE _____

_____

_____

DISTANCE _____ TIME ON THE WATER _____

NOTES

_____

_____

_____

_____

_____

_____

_____

_____

_____

_____

_____

_____

_____

_____

_____

_____

_____

_____

_____

JOURNEY NAME _____

START DATE _____ END DATE _____

COMPANIONS _____

_____

_____

LOCATION _____

WEATHER CONDITIONS _____

_____

TRIP GOALS _____

_____

ROUTE _____

_____

_____

DISTANCE _____ TIME ON THE WATER _____

NOTES

_____

_____

_____

_____

_____

_____

_____

_____

_____

_____

_____

_____

_____

_____

_____

_____

_____

_____

JOURNEY NAME _____

START DATE _____ END DATE _____

COMPANIONS _____
_____
_____

LOCATION _____

WEATHER CONDITIONS _____
_____

TRIP GOALS _____
_____

ROUTE _____
_____
_____

DISTANCE _____ TIME ON THE WATER _____

NOTES

JOURNEY NAME _____

START DATE _____ END DATE _____

COMPANIONS _____

_____

_____

LOCATION _____

WEATHER CONDITIONS _____

_____

TRIP GOALS _____

_____

ROUTE _____

_____

_____

DISTANCE _____ TIME ON THE WATER _____

NOTES

JOURNEY NAME _____

START DATE _____ END DATE _____

COMPANIONS _____
_____
_____

LOCATION _____

WEATHER CONDITIONS _____
_____

TRIP GOALS _____
_____

ROUTE _____
_____
_____

DISTANCE _____ TIME ON THE WATER _____

NOTES

JOURNEY NAME _____

START DATE _____   END DATE _____

COMPANIONS _____
_____
_____

LOCATION _____

WEATHER CONDITIONS _____
_____

TRIP GOALS _____
_____

ROUTE _____
_____
_____

DISTANCE _____   TIME ON THE WATER _____

NOTES

_____
_____
_____
_____
_____
_____
_____
_____
_____
_____
_____
_____
_____
_____
_____
_____
_____
_____
_____

JOURNEY NAME _____

START DATE _____   END DATE _____

COMPANIONS _____

_____

_____

LOCATION _____

WEATHER CONDITIONS _____

_____

TRIP GOALS _____

_____

ROUTE _____

_____

_____

DISTANCE _____   TIME ON THE WATER _____

NOTES

_____
_____
_____
_____
_____
_____
_____
_____
_____
_____
_____
_____
_____
_____
_____
_____
_____
_____

JOURNEY NAME _____

START DATE _____ END DATE _____

COMPANIONS _____

_____

_____

LOCATION _____

WEATHER CONDITIONS _____

_____

TRIP GOALS _____

_____

ROUTE _____

_____

_____

DISTANCE _____ TIME ON THE WATER _____

NOTES

_____
_____
_____
_____
_____
_____
_____
_____
_____
_____
_____

_____
_____
_____
_____
_____
_____
_____
_____

JOURNEY NAME _____

START DATE _____ END DATE _____

COMPANIONS _____

_____

_____

LOCATION _____

WEATHER CONDITIONS _____

_____

TRIP GOALS _____

_____

ROUTE _____

_____

_____

DISTANCE _____ TIME ON THE WATER _____

NOTES

JOURNEY NAME _____

START DATE _____ END DATE _____

COMPANIONS _____

_____

_____

LOCATION _____

WEATHER CONDITIONS _____

_____

TRIP GOALS _____

_____

ROUTE _____

_____

_____

DISTANCE _____ TIME ON THE WATER _____

NOTES

JOURNEY NAME _____

START DATE _____ END DATE _____

COMPANIONS _____

_____

_____

LOCATION _____

WEATHER CONDITIONS _____

_____

TRIP GOALS _____

_____

ROUTE _____

_____

_____

DISTANCE _____ TIME ON THE WATER _____

NOTES

JOURNEY NAME _____

START DATE _____   END DATE _____

COMPANIONS _____

_____

_____

LOCATION _____

WEATHER CONDITIONS _____

_____

TRIP GOALS _____

_____

ROUTE _____

_____

_____

DISTANCE _____   TIME ON THE WATER _____

NOTES

JOURNEY NAME _____

START DATE _____   END DATE _____

COMPANIONS _____
_____
_____

LOCATION _____

WEATHER CONDITIONS _____
_____

TRIP GOALS _____
_____

ROUTE _____
_____
_____

DISTANCE _____   TIME ON THE WATER _____

NOTES

_____
_____
_____
_____
_____
_____
_____
_____
_____
_____
_____
_____
_____
_____
_____
_____
_____
_____

JOURNEY NAME _____

START DATE _____ END DATE _____

COMPANIONS _____

_____

_____

LOCATION _____

WEATHER CONDITIONS _____

_____

TRIP GOALS _____

_____

ROUTE _____

_____

_____

DISTANCE _____ TIME ON THE WATER _____

NOTES

JOURNEY NAME _____

START DATE _____   END DATE _____

COMPANIONS _____

_____

_____

LOCATION _____

WEATHER CONDITIONS _____

_____

TRIP GOALS _____

_____

ROUTE _____

_____

_____

DISTANCE _____   TIME ON THE WATER _____

NOTES

_____
_____
_____
_____
_____
_____
_____
_____
_____
_____
_____
_____
_____
_____
_____
_____
_____
_____

JOURNEY NAME _____

START DATE _____   END DATE _____

COMPANIONS _____

_____

_____

LOCATION _____

WEATHER CONDITIONS _____

_____

TRIP GOALS _____

_____

ROUTE _____

_____

_____

DISTANCE _____   TIME ON THE WATER _____

NOTES

_____

_____

_____

_____

_____

_____

_____

_____

_____

_____

_____

JOURNEY NAME _____

START DATE _____ END DATE _____

COMPANIONS _____

_____

_____

LOCATION _____

WEATHER CONDITIONS _____

_____

TRIP GOALS _____

_____

ROUTE _____

_____

_____

DISTANCE _____ TIME ON THE WATER _____

NOTES

JOURNEY NAME _____

START DATE _____   END DATE _____

COMPANIONS _____

_____

_____

LOCATION _____

WEATHER CONDITIONS _____

_____

TRIP GOALS _____

_____

ROUTE _____

_____

_____

DISTANCE _____   TIME ON THE WATER _____

NOTES

_____
_____
_____
_____
_____
_____
_____
_____
_____
_____
_____
_____

JOURNEY NAME _____

START DATE _____ END DATE _____

COMPANIONS _____

_____

_____

LOCATION _____

WEATHER CONDITIONS _____

_____

TRIP GOALS _____

_____

ROUTE _____

_____

_____

DISTANCE _____ TIME ON THE WATER _____

NOTES

_____

_____

_____

_____

_____

_____

_____

_____

_____

_____

_____

_____

_____

_____

_____

_____

_____

_____

JOURNEY NAME _____

START DATE _____ END DATE _____

COMPANIONS _____

_____

_____

LOCATION _____

WEATHER CONDITIONS _____

_____

TRIP GOALS _____

_____

ROUTE _____

_____

_____

DISTANCE _____ TIME ON THE WATER _____

NOTES

_____
_____
_____
_____
_____
_____
_____
_____
_____
_____
_____
_____
_____
_____
_____
_____
_____
_____
_____
_____

JOURNEY NAME _____

START DATE _____ END DATE _____

COMPANIONS _____

_____

_____

LOCATION _____

WEATHER CONDITIONS _____

_____

TRIP GOALS _____

_____

ROUTE _____

_____

_____

DISTANCE _____ TIME ON THE WATER _____

NOTES

_____

_____

_____

_____

_____

_____

_____

_____

_____

_____

_____

_____

_____

_____

_____

_____

_____

_____

JOURNEY NAME _____

START DATE _____ END DATE _____

COMPANIONS _____

_____

_____

LOCATION _____

WEATHER CONDITIONS _____

_____

TRIP GOALS _____

_____

ROUTE _____

_____

_____

DISTANCE _____ TIME ON THE WATER _____

NOTES

JOURNEY NAME _____

START DATE _____   END DATE _____

COMPANIONS _____
_____
_____

LOCATION _____

WEATHER CONDITIONS _____
_____

TRIP GOALS _____
_____

ROUTE _____
_____
_____

DISTANCE _____   TIME ON THE WATER _____

NOTES

_____
_____
_____
_____
_____
_____
_____
_____
_____
_____
_____
_____
_____
_____
_____
_____
_____
_____

JOURNEY NAME _____

START DATE _____   END DATE _____

COMPANIONS _____

_____

_____

LOCATION _____

WEATHER CONDITIONS _____

_____

TRIP GOALS _____

_____

ROUTE _____

_____

_____

DISTANCE _____   TIME ON THE WATER _____

NOTES

JOURNEY NAME _____

START DATE _____ END DATE _____

COMPANIONS _____

_____

_____

LOCATION _____

WEATHER CONDITIONS _____

_____

TRIP GOALS _____

_____

ROUTE _____

_____

_____

DISTANCE _____ TIME ON THE WATER _____

NOTES

JOURNEY NAME _____

START DATE _____ END DATE _____

COMPANIONS _____
_____
_____

LOCATION _____

WEATHER CONDITIONS _____
_____

TRIP GOALS _____
_____

ROUTE _____
_____
_____

DISTANCE _____ TIME ON THE WATER _____

NOTES

_____
_____
_____
_____
_____
_____
_____
_____
_____
_____

JOURNEY NAME _____

START DATE _____ END DATE _____

COMPANIONS _____

_____

_____

LOCATION _____

WEATHER CONDITIONS _____

_____

TRIP GOALS _____

_____

ROUTE _____

_____

_____

DISTANCE _____ TIME ON THE WATER _____

NOTES

_____
_____
_____
_____
_____
_____
_____
_____
_____
_____
_____
_____
_____
_____
_____
_____
_____
_____

JOURNEY NAME _____

START DATE _____   END DATE _____

COMPANIONS _____
_____
_____

LOCATION _____

WEATHER CONDITIONS _____
_____

TRIP GOALS _____
_____

ROUTE _____
_____
_____

DISTANCE _____   TIME ON THE WATER _____

NOTES

JOURNEY NAME _____

START DATE _____ END DATE _____

COMPANIONS _____

_____

_____

LOCATION _____

WEATHER CONDITIONS _____

_____

TRIP GOALS _____

_____

ROUTE _____

_____

_____

DISTANCE _____ TIME ON THE WATER _____

NOTES

_____
_____
_____
_____
_____
_____
_____
_____
_____
_____
_____
_____
_____
_____
_____
_____
_____
_____
_____

JOURNEY NAME _____

START DATE _____ END DATE _____

COMPANIONS _____
_____
_____

LOCATION _____

WEATHER CONDITIONS _____
_____

TRIP GOALS _____
_____

ROUTE _____
_____
_____

DISTANCE _____ TIME ON THE WATER _____

NOTES

_____
_____
_____
_____
_____
_____
_____
_____
_____
_____
_____

_____
_____
_____
_____
_____
_____
_____
_____

JOURNEY NAME _____

START DATE _____ END DATE _____

COMPANIONS _____

_____

_____

LOCATION _____

WEATHER CONDITIONS _____

_____

TRIP GOALS _____

_____

ROUTE _____

_____

_____

DISTANCE _____ TIME ON THE WATER _____

NOTES

_____
_____
_____
_____
_____
_____
_____
_____
_____
_____
_____
_____
_____
_____
_____
_____
_____
_____
_____

JOURNEY NAME _____

START DATE _____ END DATE _____

COMPANIONS _____

_____

_____

LOCATION _____

WEATHER CONDITIONS _____

_____

TRIP GOALS _____

_____

ROUTE _____

_____

_____

DISTANCE _____ TIME ON THE WATER _____

NOTES

_____

_____

_____

_____

_____

_____

_____

_____

_____

_____

_____

_____

_____

_____

_____

_____

_____

_____

_____

_____

JOURNEY NAME _____

START DATE _____   END DATE _____

COMPANIONS _____

_____

_____

LOCATION _____

WEATHER CONDITIONS _____

_____

TRIP GOALS _____

_____

ROUTE _____

_____

_____

DISTANCE _____   TIME ON THE WATER _____

NOTES

JOURNEY NAME _____

START DATE _____   END DATE _____

COMPANIONS _____

_____

_____

LOCATION _____

WEATHER CONDITIONS _____

_____

TRIP GOALS _____

_____

ROUTE _____

_____

_____

DISTANCE _____   TIME ON THE WATER _____

NOTES

JOURNEY NAME _____

START DATE _____ END DATE _____

COMPANIONS _____
_____
_____

LOCATION _____

WEATHER CONDITIONS _____
_____

TRIP GOALS _____
_____

ROUTE _____
_____
_____

DISTANCE _____ TIME ON THE WATER _____

NOTES

JOURNEY NAME _____

START DATE _____ END DATE _____

COMPANIONS _____

_____

_____

LOCATION _____

WEATHER CONDITIONS _____

_____

TRIP GOALS _____

_____

ROUTE _____

_____

_____

DISTANCE _____ TIME ON THE WATER _____

NOTES

_____

_____

_____

_____

_____

_____

_____

_____

_____

_____

_____

                      _____

                      _____

                      _____

                      _____

                      _____

                      _____

                      _____

                      _____

JOURNEY NAME _____

START DATE _____ END DATE _____

COMPANIONS _____

_____

_____

LOCATION _____

WEATHER CONDITIONS _____

_____

TRIP GOALS _____

_____

ROUTE _____

_____

_____

DISTANCE _____ TIME ON THE WATER _____

NOTES

_____

_____

_____

_____

_____

_____

_____

_____

_____

_____

_____

_____

_____

_____

_____

_____

_____

_____

JOURNEY NAME _____

START DATE _____   END DATE _____

COMPANIONS _____

_____

_____

LOCATION _____

WEATHER CONDITIONS _____

_____

TRIP GOALS _____

_____

ROUTE _____

_____

_____

DISTANCE _____   TIME ON THE WATER _____

NOTES

_____

_____

_____

_____

_____

_____

_____

_____

_____

_____

_____

_____

_____

_____

_____

_____

_____

_____

_____

JOURNEY NAME _____

START DATE _____ END DATE _____

COMPANIONS _____

_____

_____

LOCATION _____

WEATHER CONDITIONS _____

_____

TRIP GOALS _____

_____

ROUTE _____

_____

_____

DISTANCE _____ TIME ON THE WATER _____

NOTES

_____

_____

_____

_____

_____

_____

_____

_____

_____

_____

_____

_____

_____

_____

_____

_____

_____

_____

_____

JOURNEY NAME _____

START DATE _____   END DATE _____

COMPANIONS _____

_____

_____

LOCATION _____

WEATHER CONDITIONS _____

_____

TRIP GOALS _____

_____

ROUTE _____

_____

_____

DISTANCE _____   TIME ON THE WATER _____

NOTES

JOURNEY NAME _____

START DATE _____   END DATE _____

COMPANIONS _____

_____

_____

LOCATION _____

WEATHER CONDITIONS _____

_____

TRIP GOALS _____

_____

ROUTE _____

_____

_____

DISTANCE _____   TIME ON THE WATER _____

NOTES

JOURNEY NAME _____

START DATE _____ END DATE _____

COMPANIONS _____

_____

_____

LOCATION _____

WEATHER CONDITIONS _____

_____

TRIP GOALS _____

_____

ROUTE _____

_____

_____

DISTANCE _____ TIME ON THE WATER _____

NOTES

JOURNEY NAME _____

START DATE _____ END DATE _____

COMPANIONS _____

_____

_____

LOCATION _____

WEATHER CONDITIONS _____

_____

TRIP GOALS _____

_____

ROUTE _____

_____

_____

DISTANCE _____ TIME ON THE WATER _____

NOTES

_____

_____

_____

_____

_____

_____

_____

_____

_____

_____

_____

_____

_____

_____

_____

_____

_____

_____

JOURNEY NAME _____

START DATE _____   END DATE _____

COMPANIONS _____

_____

_____

LOCATION _____

WEATHER CONDITIONS _____

_____

TRIP GOALS _____

_____

ROUTE _____

_____

_____

DISTANCE _____   TIME ON THE WATER _____

NOTES

JOURNEY NAME _____

START DATE _____   END DATE _____

COMPANIONS _____
_____
_____

LOCATION _____

WEATHER CONDITIONS _____
_____

TRIP GOALS _____
_____

ROUTE _____
_____
_____

DISTANCE _____   TIME ON THE WATER _____

NOTES

JOURNEY NAME _____

START DATE _____   END DATE _____

COMPANIONS _____

_____

_____

LOCATION _____

WEATHER CONDITIONS _____

_____

TRIP GOALS _____

_____

ROUTE _____

_____

_____

DISTANCE _____   TIME ON THE WATER _____

NOTES

JOURNEY NAME _____

START DATE _____   END DATE _____

COMPANIONS _____

_____

_____

LOCATION _____

WEATHER CONDITIONS _____

_____

TRIP GOALS _____

_____

ROUTE _____

_____

_____

DISTANCE _____   TIME ON THE WATER _____

NOTES

JOURNEY NAME _____
START DATE _____   END DATE _____
COMPANIONS _____
_____
_____
LOCATION _____
WEATHER CONDITIONS _____
_____
TRIP GOALS _____
_____
ROUTE _____
_____
_____
DISTANCE _____   TIME ON THE WATER _____

NOTES

JOURNEY NAME _____

START DATE _____ END DATE _____

COMPANIONS _____

_____

_____

LOCATION _____

WEATHER CONDITIONS _____

_____

TRIP GOALS _____

_____

ROUTE _____

_____

_____

DISTANCE _____ TIME ON THE WATER _____

NOTES

_____

_____

_____

_____

_____

_____

_____

_____

_____

_____

_____

_____

_____

_____

_____

_____

_____

JOURNEY NAME _____

START DATE _____ END DATE _____

COMPANIONS _____

_____

_____

LOCATION _____

WEATHER CONDITIONS _____

_____

TRIP GOALS _____

_____

ROUTE _____

_____

_____

DISTANCE _____ TIME ON THE WATER _____

NOTES

JOURNEY NAME _____

START DATE _____ END DATE _____

COMPANIONS _____

_____

_____

LOCATION _____

WEATHER CONDITIONS _____

_____

TRIP GOALS _____

_____

ROUTE _____

_____

_____

DISTANCE _____ TIME ON THE WATER _____

NOTES

JOURNEY NAME _____

START DATE _____   END DATE _____

COMPANIONS _____

_____

_____

LOCATION _____

WEATHER CONDITIONS _____

_____

TRIP GOALS _____

_____

ROUTE _____

_____

_____

DISTANCE _____   TIME ON THE WATER _____

NOTES

JOURNEY NAME _____

START DATE _____ END DATE _____

COMPANIONS _____
_____
_____

LOCATION _____

WEATHER CONDITIONS _____
_____

TRIP GOALS _____
_____

ROUTE _____
_____
_____

DISTANCE _____ TIME ON THE WATER _____

NOTES

JOURNEY NAME _____

START DATE _____ END DATE _____

COMPANIONS _____
_____
_____

LOCATION _____

WEATHER CONDITIONS _____
_____

TRIP GOALS _____
_____

ROUTE _____
_____
_____

DISTANCE _____ TIME ON THE WATER _____

NOTES

JOURNEY NAME _____
START DATE _____ END DATE _____
COMPANIONS _____
_____
_____

LOCATION _____
WEATHER CONDITIONS _____
_____

TRIP GOALS _____
_____

ROUTE _____
_____
_____

DISTANCE _____ TIME ON THE WATER _____

NOTES

_____
_____
_____
_____
_____
_____
_____
_____
_____
_____
_____
_____
_____
_____
_____
_____
_____
_____
_____

JOURNEY NAME _____

START DATE _____   END DATE _____

COMPANIONS _____

_____

_____

LOCATION _____

WEATHER CONDITIONS _____

_____

TRIP GOALS _____

_____

ROUTE _____

_____

_____

DISTANCE _____   TIME ON THE WATER _____

NOTES

_____
_____
_____
_____
_____
_____
_____
_____
_____
_____
_____
_____

JOURNEY NAME _____

START DATE _____ END DATE _____

COMPANIONS _____
_____
_____

LOCATION _____

WEATHER CONDITIONS _____
_____

TRIP GOALS _____
_____

ROUTE _____
_____
_____

DISTANCE _____ TIME ON THE WATER _____

NOTES

JOURNEY NAME _____

START DATE _____   END DATE _____

COMPANIONS _____

_____

_____

LOCATION _____

WEATHER CONDITIONS _____

_____

TRIP GOALS _____

_____

ROUTE _____

_____

_____

DISTANCE _____   TIME ON THE WATER _____

NOTES

_____

_____

_____

_____

_____

_____

_____

_____

_____

_____

_____

_____

_____

_____

_____

_____

_____

_____

_____

JOURNEY NAME _____

START DATE _____ END DATE _____

COMPANIONS _____
_____
_____

LOCATION _____

WEATHER CONDITIONS _____
_____

TRIP GOALS _____
_____

ROUTE _____
_____
_____

DISTANCE _____ TIME ON THE WATER _____

NOTES

_____
_____
_____
_____
_____
_____
_____
_____
_____
_____
_____
_____
_____
_____
_____
_____
_____
_____

JOURNEY NAME _____

START DATE _____ END DATE _____

COMPANIONS _____

_____

_____

LOCATION _____

WEATHER CONDITIONS _____

_____

TRIP GOALS _____

_____

ROUTE _____

_____

_____

DISTANCE _____ TIME ON THE WATER _____

NOTES

_____

_____

_____

_____

_____

_____

_____

_____

_____

_____

_____

_____

_____

_____

_____

_____

_____

JOURNEY NAME _____

START DATE _____ END DATE _____

COMPANIONS _____

_____

_____

LOCATION _____

WEATHER CONDITIONS _____

_____

TRIP GOALS _____

_____

ROUTE _____

_____

_____

DISTANCE _____ TIME ON THE WATER _____

NOTES

_____
_____
_____
_____
_____
_____
_____
_____
_____
_____
_____
_____
_____
_____
_____
_____
_____
_____
_____

JOURNEY NAME _____

START DATE _____ END DATE _____

COMPANIONS _____

_____

_____

LOCATION _____

WEATHER CONDITIONS _____

_____

TRIP GOALS _____

_____

ROUTE _____

_____

_____

DISTANCE _____ TIME ON THE WATER _____

NOTES

_____

_____

_____

_____

_____

_____

_____

_____

_____

_____

_____

_____

_____

_____

_____

_____

_____

_____

JOURNEY NAME _____

START DATE _____   END DATE _____

COMPANIONS _____
_____
_____

LOCATION _____

WEATHER CONDITIONS _____
_____

TRIP GOALS _____
_____

ROUTE _____
_____
_____

DISTANCE _____   TIME ON THE WATER _____

NOTES

JOURNEY NAME _____

START DATE _____   END DATE _____

COMPANIONS _____

_____

_____

LOCATION _____

WEATHER CONDITIONS _____

_____

TRIP GOALS _____

_____

ROUTE _____

_____

_____

DISTANCE _____   TIME ON THE WATER _____

NOTES

Printed in Great Britain
by Amazon